WITHDRAWN

The
BUTTERFLY
Alphabet Book

by Brian Cassie and Jerry Pallotta

illustrated by Mark Astrella

 Charlesbridge

Written especially for the Maine ladies:
Mary Giard, Ruth Davison, and Donna Maxim

— *Jerry Pallotta*
Peggotty Beach, 1995

To my wonderful family
— *Brian Cassie*

Thank you, Mom, for supporting my art career.
— *Mark Astrella*

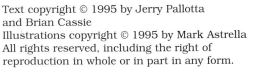

Text copyright © 1995 by Jerry Pallotta
and Brian Cassie
Illustrations copyright © 1995 by Mark Astrella

Published by
Charlesbridge Publishing
85 Main Street, Watertown, MA 02472-4411
(617) 926-0329
www.charlesbridge.com

Printed in the United States of America
(sc)   10   9   8   7   6
(hc)   10   9   8   7   6   5   4

Printed on Recycled Paper

Library of Congress Cataloging-in-Publication Data
Cassie, Brian, 1953–
     The butterfly alphabet book / by Brian Cassie
and Jerry Pallotta; illustrated by Mark Astrella.
          p.   cm.
     ISBN 0-88106-895-0 (reinforced for library use)
     ISBN 0-88106-894-2 (softcover)
     1. Butterflies—Juvenile literature. 2. English
language—Alphabet—Juvenile literature. [1. Butterflies. 2. Alphabet.] I. Pallotta, Jerry. II. Astrella,
Mark, ill. III. Title.
QL544.2.C38   1995
595.78'9 — dc20
[E]
                                        95-7066
                                          CIP
                                          AC

Books by Jerry Pallotta:
The Icky Bug Alphabet Book
The Icky Bug Counting Book
The Bird Alphabet Book
The Ocean Alphabet Book
The Flower Alphabet Book
The Yucky Reptile Alphabet Book
The Frog Alphabet Book
The Furry Animal Alphabet Book
The Dinosaur Alphabet Book
The Underwater Alphabet Book
The Victory Garden Vegetable Alphabet Book
The Extinct Alphabet Book
The Desert Alphabet Book
The Spice Alphabet Book
The Freshwater Alphabet Book
The Airplane Alphabet Book
The Boat Alphabet Book
Going Lobstering
Cuenta los insectos (The Icky Bug Counting Book)
The Crayon Counting Book
The Crayon Counting Board Book

A a

A is for Apollo.
Apollo butterflies are the
high-flying champions of
the butterfly world. They have
been seen almost four miles
up in the mountains of Asia.

Bb

B is for Baltimore Checkerspot. If you have ever played checkers, then you probably already know how the checkerspot butterflies got their name. This butterfly has the same colors as the Baltimore Oriole bird and the Baltimore Orioles baseball team — orange, black, and white.

Cc

C is for Cracker. Have you ever heard a noisy butterfly? Crackers usually fly without making a sound. When disturbed, though, these butterflies make cracking sounds with their wings.

D d

D is for Dogface. When it is flying in a meadow, the Dogface looks like many other yellow butterflies. But when it lands, the poodle faces on its wings are easy to see.

Nobody knows how these beautiful insects got the name "Butterfly." Do *you* know?

E e

E is for Eastern Comma. This butterfly loves a sunny spot in the woods. When it folds its wings, you can see a comma on its underside. There is another butterfly called a Question Mark, but we could not find one named an Exclamation Point or a Period.

Ff

F is for Falcate Orangetip. Some butterflies have hard names to remember but not the Orangetips. Orangetips fly in the springtime before most other butterflies. The word *falcate* means its wings are curved and pointed. Take a look.

G is for Great Purple Hairstreak. All kinds of hairstreaks and other beautiful butterflies love small flowers that grow in clusters — like the lantana on this page. Planting especially to attract butterflies is called "butterfly gardening."

G g

Hh

H is for Harvester. This picture has two Harvester butterflies and two Harvester caterpillars. Where are the caterpillars? Believe it or not, they are under the white fuzzy stuff, which is really a lot of small bugs called woolly aphids. Harvester caterpillars don't eat leaves, they eat the aphids they hide under.

I i

I is for Indian Leaf Butterfly. The Indian Leaf Butterfly is perfectly camouflaged. Can you find it? It looks like a leaf on a twig, but you could walk by and never notice it.

Jj

J is for Jezabel. Jezabels
do not like to blend in.
Many kinds of Jezabels
brighten the roadside in
Australia with their red,
yellow, black, and white wings.

K k

K is for Kamehameha.
Hawaii is the only home of
the Kamehameha butterfly.
It is named after a famous
Hawaiian king.

L1

L is for Life Cycle. The life cycle of every butterfly begins with an egg being laid on the surface of a plant. Almost all female butterflies lay their eggs on certain preferred plants.

The Gulf Fritillary lays eggs only on the leaves of a passionflower vine. Its caterpillar hatches from the egg and begins eating the leaf on which it was born.

After growing and shedding its skin several times, the caterpillar pupates into a chrysalis.

Before long, the adult Gulf Fritillary emerges from the chrysalis to start the cycle all over.

Ll

L is also for Lady Slipper. Deep in the tropical rain forest, Lady Slippers fly along shady forest trails. Lady Slippers almost always fly within a few inches of the forest floor.

M is for Magdalena Alpine. High up in the Rocky Mountains, we find this all black butterfly! Because the color white reflects light and the color black absorbs light, the Magdalena Alpine's black wings keep it warm.

Mm

Nn

N is for Narcissus Jewel. What a beauty! Narcissus Jewels love to chase one another around their home in the mangrove trees. Thick mangroves are a great place to play hide-and-seek.

O is for Owl Butterfly. The Owl Butterfly's huge eyespots give it an owl face look. Owl Butterflies are not attracted to sunshine, but they are very attracted to fruit.

Oo

Pp

P is for Painted Lady. These butterflies are found in open areas on every continent except Antarctica. They have been seen a thousand miles at sea and they have even been seen in the tundra. Painted Ladies migrate from deserts every spring.

Qq

Q is for Queen
Alexandra Birdwing.
Of the twenty thousand
or so known species of
butterflies that exist in the
world, this is the largest.
This butterfly painting
is its actual size.

Rr

R is for Regal Fritillary. This handsome butterfly is endangered. Its prairie home is disappearing. Lepidopterists, scientists who study butterflies, are trying to save the Regal Fritillary by saving the prairies. Hopefully, it will not become extinct. Maybe you can help.

S s

S is for Snout. A Snout
butterfly looks like it has a
long nose. Butterflies do not
have noses. They smell with
their antennae. How would
you like a Snout on your
snout, or two antennae
on your head?

S s

S is also for Scales. Butterfly wings are covered with thousands of tiny scales. This is a close-up picture of a few. The scales overlap each other and help hold the wings together. Many scales have rainbow colors.

T is for Transparent.
Transparent butterflies have
see-through wings.
In their rain forest
home, they are
almost invisible. You could
read this book while
looking through a
Transparent.

Tt

If you think this is a butterfly, you have been fooled.

This is the Urania Moth. It flies during the day and is brightly colored like many other butterflies, but look closely. Moth antennae end in points. Almost all butterfly antennae end in little bumps called clubs.

U is for Ulysses.
Ulysses butterflies are
attracted to bright blue
objects. When butterfly
watchers swing a piece
of blue paper on the end
of a stick, the Ulysses
might think it is
another Ulysses and
fly closer for a
better look.

U u

V v

V is for Violet Copper. Most coppers are about the size and color of a copper penny. That is how they got their name. The Violet Copper is a copper of a different color!

W w

W is for Western Pygmy Blue. If you want to see a Western Pygmy Blue, you have to look very, very hard. This is the smallest butterfly in the world. With their wings open, it would take three Western Pygmy Blues to cover a dime.

No 2

X x

X is for Xami Hairstreak. American butterfly watchers will travel a long way to see a Xami Hairstreak. It just barely comes into the United States in Texas and Arizona. This butterfly is easier to find in Mexico.

Butterflies are insects. All insects have six legs. If some butterflies in this book appear to have only four legs, it is because the front two are very tiny.

Yy

Y is for Yellow Angled Sulphur.
All butterflies have two fore wings and two
hind wings. That's a total of four wings!
Butterfly wings have uppersides and
undersides that are usually entirely different
colors. Can you find the two Yellow Angled
Sulphur butterflies in this illustration?

Z z

Z is for Zephyr Metalmark. Many metalmarks have gold or silver marks on their wings that look like bright metallic specks.

Now that you have read this book, look around your neighborhood and find a zillion butterflies. Look and enjoy, but be careful, butterflies are fragile.